Dear Parent:

Congratulations! Your child is taking the first steps on an exciting journey. The destination? Independent reading!

STEP INTO READING® will help your child get there. The program offers five steps to reading success. Each step includes fun stories and colorful art. There are also Step into Reading Sticker Books, Step into Reading Math Readers, Step into Reading Write-In Readers, Step into Reading Phonics Readers, and Step into Reading Phonics First Steps! Boxed Sets—a complete literacy program with something for every child.

Learning to Read, Step by Step!

 Ready to Read Preschool–Kindergarten
• big type and easy words • rhyme and rhythm • picture clues
For children who know the alphabet and are eager to begin reading.

 Reading with Help Preschool–Grade 1
• basic vocabulary • short sentences • simple stories
For children who recognize familiar words and sound out new words with help.

 Reading on Your Own Grades 1–3
• engaging characters • easy-to-follow plots • popular topics
For children who are ready to read on their own.

 Reading Paragraphs Grades 2–3
• challenging vocabulary • short paragraphs • exciting stories
For newly independent readers who read simple sentences with confidence.

 Ready for Chapters Grades 2–4
• chapters • longer paragraphs • full-color art
For children who want to take the plunge into chapter books but still like colorful pictures.

STEP INTO READING® is designed to give every child a successful reading experience. The grade levels are only guides. Children can progress through the steps at their own speed, developing confidence in their reading, no matter what their grade.

Remember, a lifetime love of reading starts with a single step!

For my father—
like Washington, so brave and so honest
—F.M.

For Tom and Marianne—
wonderful people, wonderful friends
—R.W.

Author acknowledgments: *Thanks to the world's greatest librarian, Liz Dobuski, for guiding me toward this story. Thanks to Caprice Serafine for her help with mastiffs. Thanks to my editor, Shana Corey, for her grace and expertise in helping to draft this story. Thanks to Diane Landolf for help with photo research. Much of the research that went into crafting this story was supported by the words of George Washington himself through his voluminous writings, available at the Library of Congress, and by James Thomas Flexner's biography* Washington: The Indispensable Man.

Photo credits: George Washington with Nelson: © Francis G. Mayer/CORBIS; Alexander Hamilton: © Archivo Iconographico, S.A./CORBIS; William Howe: © Hulton/Archive by Getty Images; note to William Howe courtesy of the Library of Congress.

www.stepintoreading.com

Educators and librarians, for a variety of teaching tools, visit us at
www.randomhouse.com/teachers

Library of Congress Cataloging-in-Publication Data
Murphy, Frank, 1952–
George Washington and the general's dog / by Frank Murphy ; illustrated by Richard Walz.
p. cm. — (Step into reading. A step 3 book.)
SUMMARY: Recounts events in the life of George Washington that focus on his fondness for animals.
ISBN 0-375-81015-3 (trade) — ISBN 0-375-91015-8 (lib. bdg.)
1. Washington, George, 1732–1799—Juvenile literature. 2. Presidents—United States—Biography—Juvenile literature. 3. Generals—United States—Biography—Juvenile literature. 4. Dogs—United States—History—18th century—Juvenile literature. 5. Human-animal relationships—United States—History—18th century—Juvenile literature. [1. Washington, George, 1732–1799. 2. Presidents. 3. Human-animal relationships.] I. Walz, Richard, ill. II. Title. III. Series: Step into reading. Step 3 book.
E312.66.M84 2003 973.4'1'092—dc21 [B] 2002015218

Printed in the United States of America 25 24 23 22 21 20 19 18 17

STEP INTO READING, RANDOM HOUSE, and the Random House colophon are registered trademarks of Random House, Inc.

STEP INTO READING®

STEP 3

George Washington
★ and the ★
General's Dog

by Frank Murphy
illustrated by Richard Walz

Random House New York

1732-1799

George Washington is one of
America's greatest heroes.
Most people know that
George was honest and brave.
But there is something
about George that people
don't always know.

George Washington *loved* animals.

George learned
to ride horses as a boy.
Sometimes he rode into town.
George rode fast,
but he never fell.
People said
he was the best rider
they had ever seen.

FREDERICKSBURG, VA.
GENERAL
STORE
FOUNDED 1728

When George grew up,
he moved to a farm
called Mount Vernon.
Every day,
George checked on
the horses and hogs.

He checked on the oxen,

mules, and sheep.

But he spent the most

time with his dogs.

George had a *lot* of dogs.

He owned thirty-six dogs

in his lifetime.

He took them hunting.

He played with them.

He even gave them cute names

like "Mopsey," "Sweetlips,"

and "Truelove."

Sometimes George
spoiled his dogs.
He let them run
around the house.
One day,
George's wife, Martha,
cooked a ham for dinner.

George's dog Vulcan
jumped up and
stole the ham—
right off the table!
Martha chased after him.
But George just laughed.

George liked being
at Mount Vernon
with Martha and the animals.
But America needed him.

America was not yet

its own country.

It was an English colony.

That means it belonged

to England.

Many American colonists

wanted to be free

from England.

So they went to war.

The war was called

the American Revolution.

The colonists chose George
to be their general.

George chose his favorite dog,

Sweetlips, to go with him.

He said goodbye

to Martha and Mount Vernon.

He jumped on

his horse, Nelson.

Then he rode into battle.

Sweetlips was right beside him.

In George's day,
soldiers often brought
dogs with them to war.
Dogs helped hunt.

Dogs helped track the way.

Dogs helped guard
against wild animals.

Best of all,
dogs were great partners!

The general of
the English army
was named William Howe.
He had a dog, too.
He also had 9,000 soldiers.
They had plenty of supplies.

George did not have
nearly as many supplies.
Sometimes his soldiers
were cold.
Sometimes they were hungry.
But they did not give up.

In the fall of 1777,

George's troops

went to Pennsylvania.

They were fighting

the English troops.

Guns fired!

RAT-A-TAT-TAT!

Cannons roared.

BOOM! BANG!

Smoke filled the air.

Finally, the fighting ended.
The English soldiers
went back to their camp.
The battle was over
for the day.

The smoke began to clear.
George noticed a dog
without a soldier.
It looked lost.
George bent down
and patted the dog's head.

The dog followed George
back to the colonists' camp.
He wagged his tail.
Whose dog is this?
wondered George.

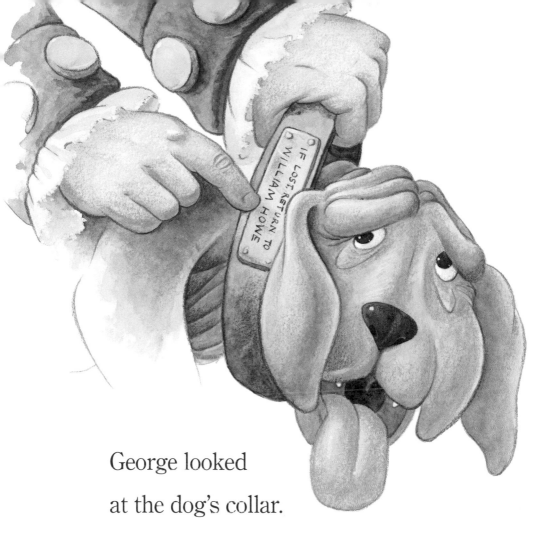

George looked
at the dog's collar.
The tag had
a man's name on it.
That name was William Howe.
William Howe!?
George couldn't believe his eyes!
William Howe was the enemy!

Word about the enemy dog
spread through camp.
Some of George's men
wanted to keep the dog.
But George said no!
George believed the dog
belonged with his master.
George had his friend
Alexander Hamilton
write a note to General Howe.
The note said that George
wanted to return the dog.

Both sides raised white flags.
The white flags meant
no one could fight.
George's soldiers
walked the dog
across the battlefield.

They gave him back

to General Howe.

LONDON CRUMPET CO. LTD.
LONDON GAZETTE
WASHINGTON RETURNS DOG
WASHINGTON
DOG

People in England
found out about
George's good deed.
The English still wanted
to beat George
and win the war.
But now they respected him.
Some English people
even liked him.
They had never heard
a story of such great kindness
between enemies.

In 1783, America won
the war against England.
America became
its very own country.
George Washington
went home to Mount Vernon.

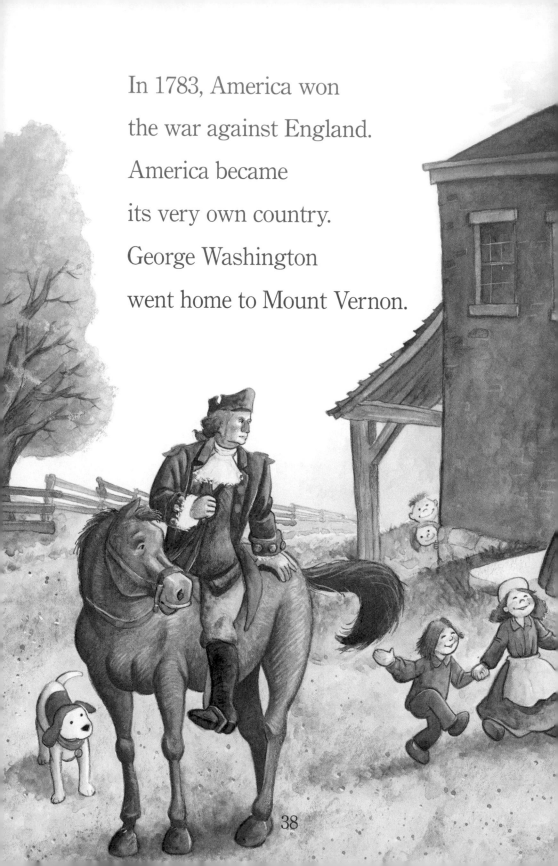

Friends around the world
wanted to honor George.
They wondered what
he would like.
Then they remembered
the story about the dog.
Soon, presents started
arriving at Mount Vernon.

To
George Washington
Mt. Vernon
Virginia

The King of Spain
sent George a mule!
George named him
"Royal Gift."

A friend from France gave George
an even bigger gift—
seven dogs!

FROM
MARQUIS DE
LAFAYETTE
TO
GEORGE WASHINGTON
MT. VERNON
VIRGINIA

George's work
was not done, though.
The American people
needed a leader.
They elected George
to be their first president.

People all over America
loved their new president.
They cheered when
he rode by in his carriage.
They knew it was him
because his six white horses
always led the way.

AUTHOR'S NOTE

The stories in this book are true. We can't be sure *exactly* how they all happened, but we've tried our best to show the way things might have been.

George Washington with Nelson

Alexander Hamilton

William Howe

Note to Sir William Howe.

General Washington's compliments to General Howe, does himself the pleasure to return him a Dog, which accidentally fell into his hands, and by the inscription on the collar, appears to belong to General Howe.

October 6th 1777

George Washington's actual letter to General Howe. It says, *"General Washington's compliments to General Howe, does himself the pleasure to return him a Dog, which accidentally fell into his hands, and by the inscription on the collar, appears to belong to General Howe."*